Gullible Greely

Greely Kirkpatrick

Publishing Coordinator – Sharon Kizziah-Holmes

Indie Pub Press
an imprint of Paperback Press, LLC.

ISBN -13: 978-1-956806-83-0

DEDICATION

To my wife, Shirley, who endured watching me agonize over writing this book.

To Dan Leyland, who encouraged me to finish the book and offered helpful Suggestions.

To the classes of 1961 and 1962, Aberdeen, Mississippi.

CONTENTS

EARLY BEGINNINGS

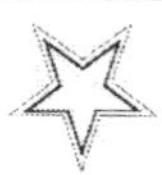

These true stories, to the best of my memory, begin in a small town, Houston, Mississippi, where I was born on June 25, 1944. My dad was overseas at the time, due to being stationed in Holland, serving his country in WWII.

A printer by trade, he fortunately avoided the front lines. My mother, Marion Halbert Kirkpatrick, sister, Brenda and I lived with my grandparents, Pete and Sadie Halbert, in Woodland, about 8 miles south of Houston. I called them DanDan and Mamaw A small man with native Indian features, he was a terrific baseball catcher.

He could reach out and grab the ball before a batter swung, or so I have been told by several people. He managed a farm in Chickasaw County for a living and just about everyone knew him. For a while in his life, alcohol was his ruler, but with God's help, he beat it. Pete loved to tell jokes. Sadie was a woman of small stature. She was strikingly beautiful and soft spoken. I recall giving her a manicure and she said I had nice hands. Mamaw wanted me to be a doctor, but I had no interest.

As I grew older, we would visit them from time to time. They lived off a gravel road in a most unusual house. Granddad wrapped the entire wooden house, which sat on concrete blocks, in a green roofing material. It came in rolls and was flexible. The cracks in the floor were so wide I could see the ground. I feared waking up with some critter joining me in bed!

The property had a well for drinking water with an enamel pan and dipper from which to drink. I always turned the dipper to some place on which the enamel had not worn off. Mom said one time, while eating supper, she noticed DanDan hadn't said much. Finally, he spoke, "Dipper, dipper, dipper, choked stiff". I can't tell you how many times we have told that story.

I guess the most disgusting thing about visiting my grandparents was the horrific smelling two-seater out-house. I gagged every time I got near it. The Sears and Roebuck catalog kept nearby did little to distract from the terrible odor.

DanDan loved Gospel music, especially the Blackwood Brothers. We would no sooner walk in the door before he took my hand and walked me to the old radio set to listen to the singing. He asked, "Bubba, do you think you could ever sing as low as the bass singer?"

The funny thing was I couldn't sing at all. I can remember walking down the gravel road to Cap Gibson's general store. They had one of those pop machines where you had to grab the top of the bottle and maneuver it through a maze to the end, then lift it up. I could hardly do it. It was fun to walk around the store and see all the goodies. I have always had a sweet tooth. Perhaps this the reason I have so many crowns. Cap's place was unique too, with all kinds of old metal signs covering the outside of his store. It was a good attention getter.

One of my aunts was Betty Jean Harrington, who also went by the nick name of "Tutter" (the "u" is short). She lived about 300 yards east of my grandparents. We would walk through a patch of woods where a path was made from years of walking. Occasionally, we would stop to smoke a grapevine. Boy, those things could burn your mouth, but they made us feel older. There were also some muscadine bushes that would give you a belly ache, if too many were eaten. They were in the grape family and had a core. They weren't my favorite, I liked plums much better.

Tutter's house was different. It had a large porch, wrapping around the house, making for lots of playing. The front steps were made of concrete with clear round balls displaying pictures of the family. They took the balls and placed them into the steps. I thought it was kind of weird at the time. I guess I still do. I suppose most families have their weirdos.

Today, many people are diagnosed with Bi-Polar disorders or OCD issues. I grew up with OCD. For years I would count to five with my fingers over and over again. I couldn't seem to stop. Very few people knew this.

Do you remember the song "Ode to Billy Joe" by Bobby Gentry? She was born in Woodland and was a one hit wonder (Ode to Billy Joe) I tell people that's my claim to fame. As kids, we liked to go to the railroad tracks west of my grandparent's house, many hours were spent walking those tracks. One of the highlights of the day was when a train would come by, and the caboose conductor would wave. We would put our ears on the rails to listen for approaching trains. Of course, we would have a contest to see who could walk on the rails the longest.

When the war was over, Dad came home and we moved to Aberdeen, Mississippi. It was about 28 miles east of Houston. For a while, we lived in the Old Judge Acker house. It was a beautiful old place with huge magnolia trees. They smelled so good I recall thinking, if something smells that great, it must taste good. Wrong. It was super bitter. The leaf had a silky feel. It is a beautiful tree and the state flower of Mississippi.

I also loved to climb them. When I was about five, I decided to climb the tallest one. My journey up came without problems. However, the way down was not so smooth. Fear started to grab me and was paralyzed. Thankfully, mother heard me yelling for help. She helped me down and I was elated to have my feet on the ground again!

Another incident happened at the Judge Acker home. It had been raining and we were playing in the water beside the front porch. Brenda pushed me down and I fell on a broken glass milk bottle. Mom rushed me to the hospital where Dr. Kennedy sewed up my left knee with 17 stitches and put my whole leg in a cast. I am pleased to brag about how my knee has not bothered me once in all these years.

Office Supplies and Printing

Dad opened the Office Supply Store on main street. We not only sold office items, but also had a number of printing presses. Our slogan was, "Nothing but the Best from the OSS." Some of my friends used to sing the jingle just to aggravate me. There were 26 steps to the second floor. We often received large cartons of paper for printing.

The guy who went up first had to walk backward. It was a real strain on the "ole" back. This one particular day I was feeling my oats. I said, "watch this," and I took a carton of 20 x 24 paper (144 lbs.) and tried to press it over my head. Falling backward on to a table, my co-workers had to remove it from my chest. It was about 3 days before I could stand up straight and about as long for my co-workers to stop laughing.

Young and dumb!

Frighteningly, the nearby furniture store caught on fire. It was the first time I experienced smoke so thick you could not breathe. There was considerable damage. Surprisingly, many people responded immediately saving thousands of dollars of merchandise. I remember Paul Stanford, a friend, working like a dog for hours. If you have never experienced the stifling smell of smoke, I can assure you it is not pleasant. Dad had good insurance and with the "fire sale," the accident worked out to our advantage.

ABERDEEN, MISSISSIPPI

Aberdeen was a sleepy town of about 5,000 people. The 6 boulevards through the city, traveled from traffic light to traffic light lined with large magnolia trees, covered in beautiful large cones. Every Christmas the city would decorate the trees with different colored lights. Quite a sight! The size of the trees with multicolored bulbs and a large star on top was a nice view for all.

The town of Aberdeen, once a year selected a number of antebellum houses gracing the town and the owners would dress up to fit the occasion. I had a friend who called them "Alabama" homes. You paid a fee and chose the house(s) you wanted to see.

Aberdeen celebrated its 150th year old birthday in 1976. We put on a pageant at the new football field. We dressed up in costumes like we were living in 1826. I thought it was awesome when a canon fired loudly and my Optometrist shouted, “Shoot low Sherman, he’s riding a Shetland.”

At Aberdeen you could play in the band and still go out for football. I played the snare drums and occasionally the bass drum. A big part of the fun was sitting by my steady girl, who played the cymbals. We would travel to nearby towns and play in their Christmas parades. It got cold in December and it was easy to drop your drum sticks. I was afraid of dropping mine, especially if I was the only drummer.

On our way to participate in a large parade in Greenwood, I looked out the window of our school bus and saw a large tire bouncing down the highway. It hit the oncoming car head on! The bus swerved and pulled off the road. The bus driver, Greg Montgomery, a student was later given an award for handling the incident exceptionally well. We were all grateful to him.

I am sorry to say Greg Montgomery died from cancer at 59. It’s tragic to lose a classmate. You have so many memories forever blazoned in your mind.

SCHOOL DAYS

At the age of five, the realization of school caused me to be nauseated. Some of you may identify with such a feeling. I was a shy kid and as some say, "afraid of my own shadow." However, I was pleasantly surprised I loved school. It was because I had a great first grade teacher, Vesta Woods was softspoken and kind. My first day of school, she had everyone stand and give their complete name. When it came my turn, I stood up and said, "Greely Cornelius Kirkpatrick the third." The only problem was I had a slight speech impediment and could not pronounce letters like "h". As a result, it came out "turd" instead of third. The room filled with laughter, and I haven't liked my name since. Besides, it is an easy name to make fun of "Greasy Corn, "Greedy Greely" or "Gullible Greely".

I also recall going to the first grade with a pillow. You can image the looks I received. I had been given a penicillin shot, which caused one side of my buttock to be twice the size of the other. When in grammar school, I was so undersized most of the girls were bigger than me. At recess I loved to play soft ball was usually chosen near the end, along with some of the stronger girls. I either played right field or backup catcher. Rarely, was a ball ever hit to right field, but playing backup catcher kept one busy running after balls the catcher missed.

Talking about grammar school, my cousin Pete Mckellar was born with a cleft pallet. He had several surgeries which helped us understand him better. But one day, when I was in the eighth grade and he was in the fourth, he came to the junior high building and found me. He proceeded to explain about this guy who was bulling him, calling him names and making fun of him. Pete asked if I would go with him to take care of the matter. While I didn't want to go, it looked like I was destined for the following incident. When we got to the building, I learned the bully was about 6 feet tall and considerably older, since he had failed several grades. When I opened my mouth, I was surprised when words came out. I asked him politely, to please leave my cousin alone. He just smiled and walked away. It was like the old Alka-Seltzer commercial, "Oh what a relief it was." Finally, reaching high school, our class (10th) voted on who would serve as officers completely caught off guard, I was elected class President. I showed my ignorance, when I asked if there were any "denominations" for Vice-president. Of course, the pictures for the yearbook were problematic for the photographer. The two other officers, being the tallest girls in school, required me to stand on the first step with the girls standing on the floor in order to appear a measly inch taller. Plum embarrassing!

BENTONITE

One of the more fun things to do was to swim in the Bentonite pits. Bentonite is a product once removed from the ground, it leaves a large body of green water. There were a number of places from which you could jump or dive. Having a fear of heights, but not wanting to be called a name, I made the forty-foot jump. I remember hitting the water. Ouch, it hurt!

David Houston was a diver. Choosing a spot 10 feet or so higher. I can see him right now making a beautiful swan dive. Several months later, we went back to check out the pits, I gasped. little did we know there was a solid slab under the water right where we had been jumping. The water level had been affected by a slow leak.

This swimming hole was not the only

dangerous one nearby. A friend of mine dove into the water without checking the depth. He stuck in the muddy bottom, paralyzing himself in the process. Those there remember him repeating a prayer continuously, "Please God, don't let me die." Lamar Rodabaugh was confined to a wheelchair for life. He was a year older than me and on occasions he would stop by and shoot some hoops.

Lamar, whose temper before the accident could be scary. Also, he rarely smiled. He completely changed afterward. He went on to attend college and became a fine high school counsellor, inspiring everyone. He always had a smile and kind words land eventually got married and had 2 children.

He asked me to speak on Career Day (this was a day of presenting information about various jobs). I spoke about the office supply and printing business. Hesitantly, I agreed. Having read the number one fear of the average person is speaking in public, I took a 3" wide roll of adding machine paper and made notes in case my mind went blank. As I began to speak, I told the class about the notes before accidently dropping the roll. It hit the floor and rolled almost to the back of the classroom. Everyone laughed, thinking it was done on purpose. That little miscue settled my nerves making it possible to continue.

When the Rodabaugh family moved, the Tovar family settled into the house. Mr. Tovar was a great man. All who knew him, admired him. He owned the local radio station WMPA. His daughter, about fourteen was paralyzed. I never knew why, never asked, but she was super smart. Incredibly, she wrote with her toes. Ashamedly, she wrote better than I could with my hands. Mr. Tovar rigged up a system where a speaker and receiver allowed her to listen and speak in class.

The radio station sponsored a Little League baseball team. They had gone 0-10 the first half of the season. The team's coach resigned because a young lad died due to a line drive to the throat. Reluctantly, I accepted the offer. Many times, while at work, the phone would ring and a small voice would ask, "Mr. Kirkpatrick, are we having practice today?" I learned the meaning of the saying "Patience is a virtue." We managed a record of 3-7 the last 10 games.

ATHLETES

Aberdeen turned out some pretty good athletes. For instance, Jimmy Walden received a football scholarship to Wyoming and made Honorable Mention All American. He also was the head coach at Washington State for several years. David Colbert also received a football scholarship to Wyoming, but it was just too far from home. He decided to work for a company named Potash, where he retired. In 1955 Molly Halbert and Jimmie Lee Dodd were co-captains of the Mississippi State football team.

Frank Halbert, Molly's brother, played running back for the Ole Miss Rebels. They nick named him "Hobby Horse" because he ran kind of funny. I attended an Ole Miss game and the PA announcer introduced Frank as #43 on your program, #1 in your heart. “Whoo hoo Mercy” the radio announcer would say.

Billy Harrington, who married my sister, Brenda on my birthday, received a basketball scholarship to Ole Miss. He was second in scoring in his freshman year. Jerrell Wilson went to the University of Southern Miss on a football scholarship and was drafted as a punter for the KC Chiefs, where he led the AFC for several years.

Terry and Jerry Sheldon (twins) went to Murray State. The coach couldn’t tell them apart, so he called them Terry “the punter” and Jerry the runner.” Two of my class mates were outstanding football players: David Houston and Fred Barron. I will have more to say about these two later.

The movie theater was a popular place. One night some guys from the football team decided to go to a scary movie. They walked, as the theater wasn’t far. Terry Sheldon told the fellows he didn’t like movies that frightened him. After the movie, one of the guys slipped ahead, hid behind a bush and jumped out with a blood curdling scream. Terry fainted! A tough football player. He was the laughing stock of the school for a few days.

Going to the movies was one of our favorite things to do. It was owned by four people, 2 sisters and 2 brothers, None of them ever married. Every time I went there, they would ask me how old I was. You see, the movie was FREE until you turned 12, then they charged you twenty-five cents. I sure hated it when it happened.

CHANGES

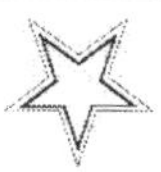

One afternoon Brenda and I walked out of the OSS and I very slowly read the Marque sign on the theater Tar-ran-tu-la. Never being the world's best speller I asked Brenda what it meant. She laughed and explained I had put the emphasis in the wrong place. It was Ta-rant-ula, like the spider. Everyone got tickled.

Another thing I always looked forward to were the Serials. They were fun and continued each week. My favorite was "Rocket Man". He wore a helmet that looked like a bullet and there were knobs on his metal vest. I can remember it like it was yesterday. I would go home, get a towel fasten it with a safety pin and jump off the front porch. Of course, there were others, "Heckle and Jeckle" always signed off saying, "See you next week with a brand-new show."

I especially enjoyed Westerns. Just when you thought the bad guys had won, the Calvary arrived! Most everyone would stand up, whistle, clap or shout. Brenda and I went to the movies one day and passed by the Ford dealership, which had a box full of puppies. An employee asked if we wanted one. We went running home as fast as we could run. Mom told us absolutely not! We began to beg (tears and all). You know how kids can be crafty. Finally, she broke down and we went back to pick one out. She was only about 3 weeks old. We thought we were going to lose her because she would not eat. Mom saved the day, when she found a baby doll's bottle. The entire family loved that mutt.

Unfortunately, she was killed by a car. I saw the whole incident. It was gut wrenching. I was surprised I didn't throw up. We called my uncle who buried her for us. My sister blamed me. You know how you can be when something tragic happens. You are hurt and mad and want to lash out at someone. Brenda said, "She would not be dead, if you had not gone to play tennis that day!" I was walking to David Dabbs's house and Penny (our dog) ran after some people. She never knew what hit her. She didn't see the car for an embankment. Our house was not a pleasant place for a number of days. Dad got us another dog. A Chiwawa we named him "Buster." Have you ever seen a Chiwawa that looked like a bulldog? This dog was all muscles. Mom was cooking a hamburger patty on one of our visits when Shirley asked if it was for supper. Mom let out a big belly and said, "No child, this is for Buster." He loved to go to the golf with dad and he would run the whole time. He was a temperamental little fellow and would wet in dad's house slippers when he got mad. Mom put him down when he was about 17. He snapped at our first born son which was a huge mistake.

THE NEIGHBORHOOD

We loved to play games and did so almost every day until dark. Many a sandlot football game was played on a vacant lot two doors from our house. After a hard-fought sandlot game of football, I came home with 2 black eyes. My mom was mad and demanded to know who attacked me. I answered, "No one. I caught a pass and headed for the end zone, when I began to stumble. Every step I took my knees hit me in my face." Some of the games we played were: Kick the Can, Red Rover, Hide and Seek, Tag, etc. It was getting dark one night when mom opened the screen door and shouted at me to come in the house. I had been jumping off my neighbor's pick-up truck. It had a fender with a jagged piece of metal sticking out. Wouldn't you know, on my last jump, I ripped my hind side to the tune of 5 stitches. Mom told me an adage, “Always mind your mother and you will never get hurt.” Of course, it is only a general statement and not to be taken as coming true every time. Then again, there was the time my cousin set up a pup tent in our front yard. We got up at the same time and he accidently stuck a knife in my right eye. Ironically, we were playing “Doctor”. Mom rushed me to the doctor, but it was not serious. It only went into the white of my eye. The doctor gave me a patch to wear for a few days. It was fun to look like a pirate.

Some of my friends were gym rats, but it never was my “thing.” We did put up a horizonal bar in the back yard and I would swing like a monkey. Truth is I almost killed myself on a number of occasions by falling off. I enjoyed track events and would set up different obstacles in the yard and invite my friends over to try their skills. You ever tried to high jump? I liked to try, but couldn’t beat anyone. A cane pole was used for the cross bar and the side poles were graduated at one-inch intervals. I often passed the time by working on my track skills. Bill Strawbridge lived directly behind me. He would see me trying to improve my limited skills in track and join me. A good friend and super good guy besides being a super good athlete. We played lots of golf in the summer (he beat me the majority of the time). At around 6’2” and 175 lbs. He was a formidable opponent. Bill played end on the football team, center on the basketball team, first base on the baseball team and made All-State as a tuba player. Bill's dad was killed in WWII. His mom had remained a widow for years, until she met Molly Halbert, Sr. I was surprised she married him because he was a cigar smoking, tobacco chewing sports nut. Mrs. Strawbridge was squeaky clean. Bill loved the Halberts and I was very happy for him.

I can certainly identify with Mr. Halbert about being a sports nut. My dad and I spent many hours playing golf. I remember playing my dad in the finals of the first flight in the club tournament About 10-15 buddies of my dad rode along and watched the match. Dad was off his game and I beat him 5 down with 4 holes to go. I felt bad about beating him so badly.

While working for dad at the OSS, but still in high school, I ran an offset printing press. I noticed the Aberdeen High school had placed an order for report cards. The wheels began to turn as I thought I could easily print a few extras. Who would know? I could put down any grade, within reason, and not have to worry about failing. Discretion was used, so as not to bring attention to the grades and end up getting caught. Everything was going great. My dad had an unusual signature, but I had it down perfectly. The cards were printed on white card stock and required a parent's signature. There was only one problem. Mrs. King (my English teacher) saw my mom at the five and dime store and they began to talk. Mom said, "I don't know why Greely made such a low grade in English." Mrs. King said, "I will tell you why he made a 58. He refused to stand before the class and quote a portion from the Canterbury Tales." Mom was confused, because I had put down a 75 on my new report card. Oops. I never imagined a conversation taking place with Mrs. King. One day she caught me in the hall and said she was serious about failing me. She won. I quoted the so-called poem. I couldn't stand the thought of another year in school.

A CRAZY TRIP

Have you ever had a friend who was a little strange? This guy (Bobby) was an Army brat and lived all over the place. He knew everything, walked like a duck and told one lie after another. He was a weird dude. He told me his teeth had no cavities because they had been coated with something which protected them. It may have protected him from cavities, but it did little to protect others from his halitosis.

Somehow, he convinced seven of us to ride our bikes to Old Waverly near Columbus, Mississippi. I was fourteen and the round trip was around twenty miles, it was a long way. The Schwinn bike helped some because it had 10 gears. We "camped" near the Tombigbee River with a railroad crossing a few hundred yards away.

The crossing had no overhead and no sides on which to walk. Someone suggested we walk to the other side. You had to watch your step because it was about 40 feet to the water. I was nervous and asked the guys, "What if a train comes?"

"Oh, don't be so negative" answered one. Another said, "Hey, don't be such a scaredy cat. Besides, I don't think this track is active anymore."

The tie tracks were spaced out so a skinny guy like me could fall right through them. There was an abandoned antebellum house not far from us. We explored inside, taking a look around. It reminded me of "Gone with the Wind." A beautiful place with a huge winding staircase of hand-crafted Mahogany wood. It was quite a sight and a trip worth taking. We never found out who the owner was, but he sure was trusting to leave the place unguarded. We left everything just like it was.

After our adventure, we headed home. Some of the guys brought food, but not my favorite, sardines, crackers, Vienna sausage and warm pop. It felt like my legs were going to fall off, so I called my mom to come and get me. The lactic acid in my body was building up and starting to hurt. Thank God for mothers!

GIRLS

I was beginning to take an interest in girls but had never kissed one. Do you remember your first kiss? A friend of mine was dating a girl, who had a younger sister, who had a crush on me. I could hardly believe it, since I barely knew her.

My buddy picked me up around seven one evening and we drove around town with our "dates". She was kind of a "happy-go-lucky" girl, but when he dropped me off at my house, as I was getting out of the back seat, she grabbed me and planted a big kiss right on my lips.

WOW! My head was spinning. I had no idea anyone would ever know we had kissed. However, the high school had a small newspaper with a section devoted to whom would you choose as your perfect boy/girl. For example, color and length of hair, eyes, nose etc. You guessed it lips like Greely Kirkpatrick. Plum embarrassing.

I didn't do a lot of dating, because girls scared me. My mom and dad never gave me the "Birds and Bees" talk. I wish I could tell you I never made any mistakes with the opposite sex, but it would not be truthful.

Mistreatment of another is often the result of jealously. I am reminded of King Saul's "insane" jealousy of David. He tried to kill David on several occasions by hurling a javelin at him. I recall a date one night where my date had been flirting with a guy at school. She was voted "Biggest Flirt" 4 years in a row.

One night, after I picked her up, I started in on her about seeing her flirting. She asked me to pull the car over. When we stopped, she vomited her supper. What an idiot I was! We dated about 2 years and most of the time, they were pleasant, except when the green-eyed monster would raise his ugly head. People thought we would surely marry, but my freshman year in college she married another guy. Looking back, I can see we would never have made it..

I believe God sent a young woman to me who was exactly what I needed. I will extol some of her finer qualities later.

SUMMER CAMP

Have you ever attended summer camp? A cute girl invited me to a camp in Pass Christian, on the Mississippi Gulf Coast. I had no idea it was a "church" camp. There were Bible classes every day with preaching every night. The experience was shocking.

Each night an invitation was offered, and my friends kept saying, "Greely, go down." I asked, "Why'?" Growing up in the Presbyterian church., I had never seen a person "go down."

I enjoyed the camp and made a lot of new friends. I was particularly excited to get to know the cute girl. It would have been nice had she attended. Later in life I became a counselor at a summer Bible camp named Green Valley near

Rogers, Arkansas. There were about 130 kids in our session. Bill McFarland was the director for many years with his wife (Kay) helping.

He was great because he was patient and had the children's best interest in mind. It was the hardest week of the year for me. I taught several classes each day, preached one night, played softball, swam and slid down on the loose rocks, as the boys' cabins were at the top of the valley.

Lights were out at 10 pm. Every night I would get my flashlight and pull the bed covers up in order to study for the upcoming Sunday. We generally got home around 2 pm on Saturday. I would stay awake about one hour and then crash. The Sunday after camp one of my elders asked me if I had a good vacation? He didn't have a clue about how exhausted I was.

SCOOTERS AND CARS

Have you ever bought a used scooter and spent most of your time trying to get it to run? Dad got me a scooter, which I rode to school quite often. This was before the purchase of the coupe. It had a lawn mower engine and never exceeded 45 miles an hour, even when going downhill. The throttle was on the right and the brakes on the left, operating by some cables and wire.

One morning, I pulled up to the stop light at school and two real scooters joined me. As usual, there were a number of kids standing behind the chain link fence waiting for the bell to ring. I remember holding the brakes and giving her full throttle. When the light changed, I shot out in front of the other two like they were standing still. I couldn't believe it worked. The kids clapping and cheering made me feel like a winner. I guess it really is true folks do pull for the underdog.

Someone named the scooter “Meat Ball.” It was an appropriate name, because I left parts of my body all over town. While it was dangerous frustratingly it also remained in the repair shop more than I rode it. Except for the grace of God, I would be dead by now. I still sport some scars from Meatball. When my sons were teenagers, they thought I was the meanest father in the world for refusing to let either of them own a motorcycle. A young friend of mine died in a crash when his motorcycle slid under a stopped school bus. He was seventeen years old with his whole life ahead of him. I may be gullible, but there are few things I pick up on quickly.

In my junior year of high school, I bought a 1952 black Plymouth coupe for $175.00. If you are familiar with that model, the trunk is the same size as the hood. It was the ugliest car at school. I tried to spruce it up by painting the rims red, adding spinners to the hub caps and putting mirrors on both sides. It had a major flaw with the gear shifts, which were 3 on the column. On occasions it would lock up in first gear. You would have to stop, raise the hood, giggle the gear rod until it was unlocked. After a while, I became frustrated and sold it for $200.00. I hope I told the new owner about the flaw, but I can’t remember. As ugly as it was, I still loved that old car.

UPGRADED HOUSE

In the offset printing business, you have to develop negatives and burn the image onto a metal plate. Dad built a "dark room" in the basement of our new (to us) house. We had moved from Highland Avenue to Davis Drive.

What a difference in the two houses. However, it was too far from our house to the OSS, so I turned the "dark room" into a small gym. I installed a speed bag, bench and weights. I enjoyed inviting friends over and laugh when they couldn't keep the speed bag going with any consistency.

Many an hour was spent in that room banging on that bag. When you are the smallest guy in your class, you have to work extra hard. I hated working out, but I was determined to get bigger.

In our basement we had a pool table. The only problem was it had a 10 inch round pipe running over the table. If you were more than 5'9", you would smack you head on it. You would not believe how many guys conked their heads and it hurt like crazy! At the time, I was about 5'7", so it never bothered me. In fact, I enjoyed seeing the faces and hearing the groans.

BASEBALL

One summer, Frank Halbert coached a Pony League baseball team. He played me at third base. We always practiced during the day, but our first game was at night. A batter fouled a ball high into the air. I shouted, "I've got it" and missed it by ten feet. A few batters later I took a line drive square in the ankle. Frank took me out of the game. He said that he was afraid I was going to get hurt. Plum embarrassing!

This, however, did not change my love for the game. In my junior year of high school, I decided to go out for the baseball season. Our first game was against Columbus, who was in the Big 8 conference. I led off and remember their pitcher being rather large. He smiled at me and threw 3 strikes. Donnie Walden was on deck. As we passed each other, he asked me, "What about the last pitch" I said, "It sounded low." My memory is fuzzy on what I said.

To this day, I don't remember what I answered, but I recall busting the front windshield from a rogue pitch in Donnie's front yard. Mr. Walden, who owned a hardware store took care of it.

One of the finest players to ever play collegiate baseball from Aberdeen was Bill Bacon. MSU gave him a scholarship to play baseball and while I didn't know Bill very well, his reputation preceded him as a mild mannered, handsome, friendly and humble young man. An asset to our baseball program. I wish I had kept his statistics for my personal interest.

Our coach had just graduated from MSU, where he played center field. Charles Dickinson was a great coach. Everyone loved him. We made it to the finals of the Little Ten conference my junior year. Would you believe Starkville's pitcher threw a no hitter and beat us 15-0. Oh, by the way, I was the last batter. My batting average was the lowest on the team. 2nd base was my position normally and coach knew I couldn't hit my way out of a wet paper bag.

MINOR SCRAPES

The abandoned railroad tracks, about 200 yards from our house, served a dual purpose: a place to run and a place of refuge. When life became difficult, I retreated to this "perfect place". Here I prayed, meditated and sometimes cried.

I drove down the old track bed not long ago and saw it had not been paved all the way. I saw myself sprinting down the track, gutting it out. My mind was flooded with memories. I checked out a pair of football cleats every summer. I hated those shoes, because they slowed me down and I was already slow enough. I felt the same about baseball cleats, so I played in my socks. If a scouting report had been done on me, it would have read "small, but slow."

A group of us guys were goofing off around the old train track, when someone noticed a heavy line (telephone, I think). It was sagging a bit so some brave soul thought he could jump, grab the line and swing to the ground. Of course, gullible Greely had to try. About the time I jumped, one of the guys threw a rock hitting me square in the top of my head. The crown of my skull.

Blood rushed down my face. I panicked and with blurred vision headed for the house. Mom was home and got a bath cloth to clean me up. We were glad it wasn't a deep wound. I wonder if my mom ever grew tired of my injuries. I know I did.

I was an accident waiting to happen. Another incident occurred when we were shooting off fireworks and I dove to keep from getting hit by one and banged my head on a concrete slab. I panicked, as usual. However, it was not serious. Of course, it wouldn't be the last encounter with concrete. I recall the blood kept getting in my eyes and hindering my vision. Fireworks were exciting to me. Sometimes I would show out and hold a small one with my fingers until it exploded. I know it was super stupid.

David Dabbs' huge front lawn created an amazing football field. However, it lacked established boundaries. The home team crossed the goal line right at the front steps. In an attempt to stop me, someone pushed me from behind. My head crashed on the concrete steps.

Blood started gushing down my face, the

thought of dying crossed my mind. A friend offered me a ride to my house on his motor scooter. Of course, he was concerned about the blood on his new jacket. He was a nice guy and I felt bad about his blood-stained jacket, but I had to hold on to something! My forehead still bears the scars from this accident.

FOOTBALL

Bill Brumley was hired as the new football coach in 1961. He was nice looking, around 6’2” and 195 lbs. He installed the “Wing-T” formation. It was a good offense, but not easy to run. Personally, I was terrible at it. Too slow to take the ball and “ride” the full back, while making a decision to leave the ball with the back or keep it and run or pass.

That year we went 5-5. I know it doesn’t make any sense, but I smoked at the time. Most people did. A few of us found an elderly lady who owned a small grocery store and would break a pack of cigarettes and sell to us for 3 for 5 cents. On the way home from football practice, we would inhale them as quickly as we could. I know I smelled like a chimney, reminding me of a little poem:

Tobacco is an Indian weed.
T'was the Devil who planted the seed.
It drains your pockets, stains your clothes
And makes a chimney of your nose.

I loved football. I did not love the hazing we received, especially the way veterans treated rookies. The product "Tuff Skin" was placed at the door leading to the practice field along with paint brushes and a pan. The objective was to paint your feet to toughen them up. It was some serious stuff!

Our well-built center shouted, "I can lift three men in one blanket with one arm." "Gullible Greely" took up the offer and was placed in the middle of a blanket with both legs firmly held by two men. One on each side. Someone took the "Tuff Skin" yanked down my pants and painted my private area. It was a dirty trick to play. That product lasted several weeks. It was one of many embarrassing mistakes I made during my football career.

The first day of practice, I went running on to the practice field when my neighbor explained my thigh pads were turned wrong. I placed them facing my groin area. Oh, yes, then there were the "fur lined" athletic supporters. They said I would be issued one for cold nights. Glad I never inquired about those despite expecting them.

The following info is about some the guys who

played football on the 1961-62 teams.

Knowing coach Brumley would kick you in the rear if you messed up a play. Bill Owings, our fullback, stated, "He better not kick me!" He was the first one to get the "boot." Those who knew what he had said were snickering behind his back, including me.

At practice on an awfully hot and humid August day, a brief shower offered relief, leaving small puddles of water behind. Bill started to lap up the water like a dog. Some memories leave an indelible imprint on the mind. One such memory was the practice just mentioned. Another was the time Bill bust through the line and ran for about 75 yards. We were cheering for him, but he fell down on the opponent's 10 yard line. There was no one near him. He just ran of gas.

For all the humorous stories I can recall, it saddens me to know Bill suffered a massive heart attack at 49 and died.

My junior year found us beginning the football season playing Corinth, who was in the Big 8 conference. Everyone was a little nervous and I think coach saw it. He gave us a big speech, "Listen men, they put their pants on just like we do, one leg at a time." However, he left out how BIG their legs were.

Our QB and his girlfriend, a cheerleader, must have been having some problems because she asked me if I would walk her to the bus, after the game. I agreed. I was so gullible I didn't stop to think how much bigger he was than me. In the process of walking her to the bus, I stepped on her foot. She tried to show no pain, but I could tell she was in pain. She limped for days.

I don't remember who came up with the idea, but several of the guys decided to dye or bleach their hair before the first game playing Columbus, who were in the B-8. Fred Barron dyed his blue. He was injured in the game and had to remove his helmet, some of the guys on the Columbus team laughed, "Look, his hair is blue." I had black hair at the time and thought gold hair would look cool. The student who did my hair at Vaugh's Beauty College left the color on too long and burned my scalp so badly there were tears running down my face. My senior picture showed some color left on the front. My mother asked me why I had my hair done. The standard answer, "Everyone else did."

Our right end, Page Box was a good person. Weighing about 175 and 6'2, he had the sharpest elbows. I declare the boy could eat a pork chop without a knife. One day during practice, the play meant for the right-wing man to get the ball, but under the circumstances, I ended up with it. Page clobbered me so painfully; I got up cussin'. Coach told me if I ever spoke like that again, he would administer the paddling himself. I thought what kind of coach won't let you say a few choice words. Page made All Little Ten in football. He married our band director's daughter, Patricia Ware. Regrettably, Page passed away from Lewy Body Syndrome.

While we are talking about coaches, there was

this one coach who would get behind me and shove me into the offensive end. It was fun for me, but I don't think the other guy appreciated it.

Our great middle linebacker (Fred Barron) had a nose for the ball. His instincts were incredible. I don't think he surpassed 5'11" 173 throughout his career. Fred went out for football, along with Amos Thompson when they were sophomores. They were the only two who had the guts to go out. I spent hours watching practice. Although it was comical to see Fred and Amos get run over by the older guys, deep down I admired them, but never told them so. The comedy started with Fred's stance, something akin to a squatting frog. It may have looked funny, but it worked for him. Fred was diverse, also playing left guard and made All Little Ten his senior year, as well as, All State Defensive Player of the year in Mississippi. At Itawamba Junior College he made All American.

Fred reminded me of the time we almost died when I saw him last year. We were on a road with loose gravel, I lost control of the truck and we did two 360's, at least it felt like that many. I jumped out and went straight to the ground thanking the Good Lord we were still alive.

BOYS

Fred, Roy Lee and I are fortunate to be alive. We were dare devils, who enjoyed pushing the envelope. I recall on the fourth of July 1961 we were cruising around Okolona, minding our own business, when some local jocals drove up beside us and shouted some obscenities. We stopped the car and arranged to meet them later that night. Returning home, we began to wonder what we had gotten ourselves into with our mouths.

Fred was the first to square off with his opponent. The guy must have weighted 300 lbs. In a matter of minutes Fred had the big guy's head pinned against a car tire. The fellow cried out, "I give up!" Roy Lee Pruett was up next. Roy was a good looking guy and he loved to fight. However, on this particular night, he was not as fortunate as Fred. His opponent's dad was a boxer.

They took their stances and Nick Daughty kicked his leg out. When Roy looked down at Nick's leg, he hit Roy square in his left cheek. He didn't go down, but you could tell it dazed him. One of the fellows came up to me and I thought I was next to fight. Thankfully, he gave me a piece of advice, "I wouldn't get involved in this if I were you". It was music to my ears. I lived by the motto, "I am a lover, not a fighter." Fred used to tease me by saying I always held their coats

Our right tackle was "Ray Baby" McGee. What a character. One night we were messing around and we decided to go across town, but Ray protested, demanding we "stop the car," so he could get out and walk to his Bemmers," (grandma)

I recall one Halloween, when a group of us walked all over town shooting off fireworks. Ray raised his right arm and shouted, "Follow me, I know this country." Please put the emphasis on the "me" and "tre." He took about 5 steps, fell down, and broke his arm. Coach Brumley was not happy. The next day, at school, Robert Martin had run into a clothesline and injured both eye lids. He looked really funny with his lids turned almost inside out. If it had been me, I would have stayed at home.

On a beautiful Saturday morning, Ray and I decided to go quail hunting without a dog. It wasn't the smartest thing to do. Not having any luck, we decided to play some one-on-one football. Ray clocked in at two hundred and fifteen pounds, while I barely tipped the scales at one hundred and twenty-five. Despite the size difference, I was giving as good as I was getting until Ray fell on my right wrist. The sound of the bone snapping will never be forgotten.

On the way home, we had to cross a fence, Ray laughed a big belly shaking guffaw after I asked him to hold my gun, "There ain't nothin' wrong with yor arm", he declared. That night, I called the girls we were supposed to have a double date with and explained the situation. Ray didn't believe until Monday morning, when I showed up a with a cast on my arm. The worse part of making it to 78 years old is watching those around you die. Ray left us while in his late 60's.

Robert Thompson moved to Aberdeen for his last two years. At practice he wore a sweatshirt that said "Hope Chest" Robert had potential, but never could "turn the corner." He made me nervous because you never knew what he was going to do. He was a good athlete. I didn't like tackling him, because he ran with his knees high. Have you ever seen "star flies?" That is what I call them. Most people say it is the last thing you see before passing out.

I had many friends throughout my lifetime, including Robert Martin, our left guard. His dad was a fine dentist, but sadly, was killed going home for lunch one day, when he turned directly into the path of an oncoming 18-wheeler.

Robert and I spent one summer cruising the street from the Rebel Inn to Ernie's Fountain Grill and back. We shared intimate details of our lives. Little did I know he would marry my high school sweetheart.

She lost her first husband in an auto accident. Lee Roy Murphee, her, ex-husband, was one who liked to live on the edge. He scared me on several occasions with his fast and reckless driving. On the night of his death, I was the last person to talk with him. Everyone told me they thought Sarah Ann and I would marry. I was deeply hurt and the wound had not healed. You probably know the saying, "Once bitten, twice shy."

Returning to the topic of football comrades. The New Albany game was at their place. We left early enough to stop and eat a hamburger. It was my debut as a 1st string defense halfback. I tried to hide my anxiousness, but have you ever tried to hide your emotions? I can't express my elation over finally starting on the A team.

During the course of the game, their quarterback threw a pass to their wide receiver. I was ready and flattened him for a loss. One of my teammates was fired up and celebrated by slamming his hands onto my shoulder pads. At half time we trailed by 7 points. Coach blamed me for not tackling their half back, who ran the ball right at me. I should have tackled him, but my vision was so poor, I didn't know he had the ball. When we went to the dressing room, the first thing coach said was, "Kirkpatrick, where were you?" I lowered my head and told everyone I didn't see the football. After the game, I asked Fred why I was the only guy he called by name. However, coach was right. I should have tackled him. We lost 19-7.

After the New Albany game, some of us went to Oxford to see the Ole Miss Rebels play on Saturday. It was a beautiful afternoon and only about a 90-mile drive. There was a huge traffic jam after the game. I made siren sounds with my mouth. Our driver, Archie Baker, pulled over. For a moment, I was worried they might make me walk home. Finally, some kind soul let us back in the line. After about 10 miles, I put my left knee against the steering wheel. Archie thought we had a flat tire and pulled off the road. Of course, we didn't but that didn't stop me from doing it again. They never invited me to another game.

I, like most people, started my football career in junior varsity, JV. We played Fulton my first game. Coach started me at right end and chose me as a co-captain. I was super nervous and realized (so I thought) I left my helmet in the dressing room. Coach Holiday was not pleased and demanded I get it NOW. Looking everywhere, I returned to the coach explaining someone must have taken it. He wrapped his knuckles on my helmet, staring at me. It was an embarrassing start.

During the game, our QB got mad about something and punched the ground, injuring his hand. Somehow, I missed the action of our QB, so I was confused when coach called me over to give me a play to run. Unaware of our missing QB, I gave coach's instructions in the huddle and lined up in the position I had been playing. Finally, someone shouted, "Hey, Greely, you are the QB." Coach had forgotten to tell me or he thought I knew what was going on. Plum embarrassing!

Continuing the debacle of this game, and before our QB hurt his hand, I told him I was wide open in the middle of the field, so throw me a jump pass. He did and our opponent's right defensive back almost cut me in two. I went back into the huddle and told him, "Don't ever let me do that again."

One of the highlights of the game was the opportunity to talk with my former 7th grade science teacher Coach Spigner. Unfortunately, the reason he now resided in Fulton was due to an accidentally discharged gun. He had shot himself and was blind. I remember walking down the steps at school when he punched me in the belly and said I needed to be playing football.

On the varsity squad our left tackle was Amos Thompson. During one game, I was sitting by a "scout" (I had injured my ankle) and saw him write down # 61 & # 71 are rough and tough. Amos was co-captain of the team and was #71. The other guy was Jimmie Lee Lusk. Amos was so popular he was voted Mr. Aberdeen High School. I never heard a negative thing about him. We eventually became such great friends we roomed together our freshman year at Southern Miss. He wasn't without his quarks though.

Have you ever seen anyone read the dictionary, when they were not looking up a word? One day, I found Amos with the dictionary. Expecting him to be looking up I word, I inquired about his search, I did not expect him to respond by explaining he was reading the dictionary to improve his language skills. Maybe this is why he passed the CPA test the first time he took it.

Amos's dad died of a massive heart attack a few days before our high school graduation. Amos was really down, as expected. When he called me and asked if I would spend graduation night with him, I accepted. Although I had plans for a date night, I was greatly relieved when my date was very understanding.

I liked the Baker boys, Archie and Dan. Both had a slight stutter, but they were great guys. Being dairy farmers, they got up early every morning. They loved having me stay the night. Looking back, I think it was just to laugh at me in a nice way. 4:30 AM is far too early for any human being to get out of a cozy bed. When we finished milking, it was time for breakfast. Squirrel or rabbit and gravy. Yum, it might be fine for a country boy, but this city slicker had to choke it down. My first school bus ride was with the Baker boys. They looked like Mutt and Jeff. The oldest, Archie weighted two hundred and five pounds, and played tackle. Dan measured in at six-three, two hundred and twenty pounds, and played guard.

In one of our JV games, the play was designed for the guard to pull to the right, but Dan forgot and pulled left. Expecting the running back to approach me, I handed Dan the ball. We were both shocked and he quickly returned the ball stuttering something. Needless to say, we lost yardage on the play.

Dan loved to wrestle in his front yard. We would try to pin each other down. He had about one hundred pounds on me, but his strength would leave him when I cheated by tickling him. Dan and I were the only two seniors to play JV football. It was more fun because it didn't really matter. I am sorry to write Dan left this world with Leukemia, while still in his 40's.

Earlier I mentioned David Houston. He lived downtown with his father, who was a lawyer. The Office Supply Store was about 2 minutes from his house at the time. In his boredom, he would come to the store asking me to come over to his place.

He was a good football player and received a scholarship to play for the Ole Miss Rebels. David and I spent a good deal of time together. He was a weightlifter. We played West Point about mid-season. They almost always had a good team. I can remember their half back fumbling the ball straight into David's arms. He made a mad dash to their end zone and scored. He was another All Little Ten member. After graduation from college, he joined the FBI and later became a Federal judge in Monroe County

Mississippi, where he continues use to serve.

One game, against Tupelo, coach told me to call 33 keep. The QB fakes, as if the play is going left before hiding the ball and running right with one guard pulling. I broke free for a sizable gain. Anyone else would have scored, but some dude caught me from behind, due to my blazing slowness. After a few more plays, coach called me over to him, snapping his fingers trying to remember my name, coach told me to call that same play. I did and they proceeded to smear me.

During the same game, I played right defensive back. Their half back broke through the line. Expecting him to score, I reached up and jerked his face mask to the ground. He got mad and I got flagged. However, it was far from my worse play. Coach called time out and explained how the QB was going to fake the ball like he was going to run, but he would pass it to their end. Stay with their left end. Their QB did exactly what coach said and I did exactly what coach said NOT to do. The QB faked a run and I tackled him, but not before he had passed the ball to his wide open end.

Maybe the toughest football game year after year was with Starkville. Consistently good, they were also bigger and faster than most teams in the conference. I wanted to play in that game so badly, but failed to hear the coach call my name to enter the game. Everyone knew how much I wanted to play and was sympathetic when I missed my chance. I could not believe I did not hear my name!

Unlike Starkville, Houston was almost always a victory for us. Funny how we remember some things from years ago and can't recall what we had for breakfast. I can see and hear clearly, coach calling the play and me handing the ball to the right wing back, who fumbled it. Coach said, "You put that ball right in his stomach. It was not your fault." I believe the wing back didn't know the play, so he didn't realize the ball was for him.

Robert Odom was our left end. He was tall, tough and could catch the ball. His only fault was being a slow runner. After a home game, he was in the backseat of a car and I didn't see his parents. I yelled out my window, "Good game, Suds." One day at practice Robert showed up after consuming some beer. He smelled like a brewery, hence earning him the name "Suds." I don't know how he could run. I would have passed out from the heat. He was somewhat aggravated with me as he pointed to his dad, who was driving the car.

While I loved football, I hated practice. My vision was terrible, which hurt my play. After every practice, we would run 40-yard wind sprints. With the sun beating down on you we were sweating like a bunch of hogs.

We had a hard running left-wing man who would run right over you. Buddy Lasky probably ran for more touchdowns than anyone on the team. He was a cool dude and never boastful. I recall he walked pushing his feet up on his toes.

Our final game was with Amory, who was our arch enemy. It was a hard-fought game. I was watching Amos and something didn't seem right. My suspicion was verified, when Amos went back to their huddle. I sat by him on the bus on the way home. He told me later he didn't remember the bus ride home.

When it came to passing the football, I was decent. The main reason I didn't complete more passes was because I couldn't see the receivers. I asked my Optometrist what my vision was. He said 20/200. What this means is, if you didn't already know, what a person with 20/20 vision sees at 200 feet, if you have 20/200 vision you see at 20 feet. During one practice, Coach asked me to throw a pass and wouldn't you know I threw a "lame duck" pass. My nerves got to me. It was then I heard coach say, "Why, he can't pass at all."

Jimmy Comer played left wing man. Some seemed to be a little jealous because his dad was successful in business. I liked Jimmy and didn't see him as being stuck up.

Carl Cooper shared playing time with Jimmy. Carl was a super nice guy. Carl's brother was in the Air Force at Columbus, MS about 30 miles away. Frequently, he would fly over Aberdeen and break the sound barrier. He did it for his mother. It was really loud!

There is a story I enjoy telling and watching the reactions of people. It goes like this: "Coach got mad at just about everyone on the team and kicked them off. Only twelve men were left. I was the twelfth man. One of the guys got hurt and coach called my name. I jumped up from the bench, grabbed my helmet and did a few wind sprints. Coach called me over and said, "Greely, go in there and tell them we are going to play with 10 men." What is funny is most people asked, "Is that really true? Did he actually do that to you?" I would laugh and answer, "Of course not."

There was a tradition at our school, where each senior left something to the school. When it came my time, I left my football jacket for Coach Brumley. I played the whole season and the seniors who didn't play so many quarters would still get a jacket. It would not have leather sleeves or the stripe across the "A." In all fairness I did not have enough playing time to receive a jacket.

It was to my chagrin everyone began to clap. I asked the person sitting by me, "What is coach doing?" He answered, "Turning red." The clapping continued. I put on a brave face and headed straight for the old railroad track. As soon as I found a comfortable place to sit down, I began to cry. The jacket, even though it didn't have leather sleeves, meant so much to me. Go ahead and call me a cry baby! I do not blame coach anymore. I was not good enough to earn it. The only letter I did earn was in golf.

On the last day of high school my junior year, four of my buddies and I cut class and drove back and forth in front of the school building.

Hollering as loud as we could, we got lots of laughs. However, at the start of the next school year on the very first day, the principal called all of us to the office. He proceeded to paddle each of us. I thought he must have let what we did simmer all summer.

BOLD MOVES

One night, I asked my parents if I could borrow the car. I think I probably drove 250 miles that night. The next morning mom asked me where I had gone. I answered that I had just ridden around town. She asked, "Then why did the car's odometer have 250 miles more after you used it?" It was to my surprise she had written down the miles on the odometer.

I suppose I got my "gullible" personality from my mother. For instance, one night at the Rebel Inn I was smoking a cigar and drinking a beer. My sister happened to be there and she told my mom. Of course, mom questioned me and I told her it must have been someone who just looked like me. She believed me.

Another time mom found a bottle of whiskey in the back of my closet. I told her it was David

Dabbs and I was only keeping it for him. On another occasion my parents went on vacation to Florida. They left my sister and me for a week. I thought, "Party Time!" I completely forgot about the neighbors. We were loud and rowdy. Naturally, word got around and I was grounded. Fred Barron denies this, but I saw him open a can of dog food and start eating it. I am not proud of my shenanigans. It seems like some folks grow up quicker than others. I was a late bloomer, physically, mentally, emotionally and spiritually.

After graduation from high school, I decided to go to St. Petersburg, FL. Some friends of mine were traveling there for a couple of weeks and staying at a relative's home. My dad's sister lived in the area and we had vacationed in St. Pete several times. I bragged about how I was going to have a great summer. The time came for my buddies to return home, but I stayed. I got a job in a large grocery store in Webb City. It wasn't another town, but it was huge enough to cover an entire block.

My dad had a life-long friend who managed the grocery part. He gave me a job as "stock boy." The hours and pay were both awful. Work started at 3:00 AM and the salary was $1.00 an hour. I rented an apartment close by and bought an old motor scooter for $45.00. My first paycheck was $66.00. When the week ended, I was exhausted, like the ole boy who said he dreamed he was a muffler and woke up exhausted.

The beaches are beautiful in that part of Florida. I was hanging out one day, when I met this really cute girl, who invited me to her house. We enjoyed one another's time together, until I asked her how old she was. Would you believe she was only 14? Oops, she sure looked a lot older. I quickly said, "Sirona," and headed for the door. When I got back to the apartment house, I began to feel like the dude who sang, "I want to go home."

I purchased a ticket to Birmingham, AL at the bus station nearby, then one to Columbus, MS. A few minutes before boarding, a voice came over the PA that a ticket had been found to Columbus. I lost it and didn't even know it. I called my mom to please come and pick me up, who was more than happy to accommodate me. She worried over me riding a cheap scooter in a fairly large city. Some of my close friends said they knew it wouldn't last. It wasn't much fun, being made fun of at my home coming.

College Days

After high school graduation, I attended 5 different colleges. I had a difficult time concentrating because my girlfriend, Sarah Ann, had married another man. It was the worst time of my life, as I could not sleep or eat much. I wasn't a Christian at the time and contemplated suicide. Sarah Ann's husband had been killed in a car accident, so everyone assumed we would marry.

My mom had been talking to a hairdresser and told her she would introduce her to me, if she would promise not to break my heart. I told mom I didn't want to date right now. Mom said the beauty shop had ordered a Dome Bookkeeping book. Her suggestion was I should hand deliver it and meet Shirley Vanlandingham. She lived at Trebloc, MS, which is Colbert spelled backward, due to the number of people named Colbert who lived there. It was about 17 miles west of Aberdeen. I reluctantly agreed and man was I glad I went.

When I opened the door Shirley smiled at me and I melted. WOW she was beautiful. It took me about 3 months to ask her out and I was hooked after the first kiss. Six months later we were married. In February we celebrated 55 years. Three years ago she had a cardiac arrest. We were at Cheddars Restaurant in Springfield, MO. Having ordered and received our salads, I asked Shirley if she felt alright. Then about that time, her face fell into her salad. I got up and took the fork out of her hand. She had a "death" grip on it. She also had a "death" rattle. I yelled for someone to call 911. It seemed like it took them forever to arrive. I young man named Stephen Chandler had been a "first responder" and understood the necessity of giving CPR correctly.

After shocking her lifeless body, they got a heartbeat and rushed her to the hospital. I was in a state of confusion. A stranger must have seen my quandary and offered to drive me to the hospital. He insisted on staying with me until some family members arrived. John Martin was his name and I learned later he was a Christian.

The Good Lord was watching out for her and me. My favorite song now is Dean Martin's old Song "Return to Me." They made a movie with this song being played throughout the show. It is an excellent movie. Shirley is the love of my life.

Whenever I am down, I think of her and all the great times we have had together.

While dating almost every night, a funny thing happened. We were going down this hill, when we decided to park and smooch a while. I owned a 1956 Oldsmobile Super 88. When it was time to go home, the car would not crank. We walked to her house (about 2 miles) and she let me take her car home. The next day a friend of mine went with me to get my car. I told him I had not been having any problems with the car. He got in and started to laugh. I had left the thing in neutral and it would only crank in park. Plum embarrassing.

A few months before we got married, I took Shirley to the Aberdeen Country Club to play golf. I opened the trunk, got my clubs and shoes out, threw my keys in the trunk and slammed it shut. I wasn't thinking straight because she was wearing a purple outfit that greatly distracted me.

There was another incident where I was distracted from my studies at MSU. I had grown extremely tired of school. It was the last semester and I was taking 21 hours to graduate. What a lame choice. It really cut down on my play time. The university was experimenting with 3 to a dorm room. Bad decision in my opinion it was ridiculously crowded.

I don't recall exactly how I made friends with Slim Hartley. He was a freshman and on the MSU basketball team. He lived in south Mississippi. He loved to shoot pool. During my final exams, Slim came by my dorm room wanting to go to the pool hall and like the song says, "You don't mess around with Slim." I told him I was in the middle of studying for 7 exams. He could care less. He picked me up and carried me to the car. Ole Slim was what you call a "good ole boy." He was a terrific basketball player, but a lousy student. He flunked out after one semester. Oh yes, he slobbered when he spoke.

I was buried in trying to prepare for finals, when a knock came on the door. A buddy said there is a good-looking woman asking for me. Shirley and I had been seeing each other and I really liked her. She had no idea how far behind I was in studying. She asked if I could take a minute and go with her for a coke. I couldn't say "no" and take the risk of ruining her interest.

By the grace of God, I got a B.S. degree in General Business. Sometimes I tell people I am proof that one can go to college, graduate and not learn anything. I don't remember ever raising my hand in any class. I went because most of my friends went. College life was a real eye opener for this small town, gullible kid. My roommate (Amos Thompson) and I thought we wanted to join a fraternity. Have you ever been through (Rush Week)? It was wild!

I think Amos and I stayed intoxicated the entire time. Both of us pledged ATO. It was mostly because of Gene Carlisle. He was from Aberdeen and went on to be a successful entrepreneur. He was also somewhat of a BMOC. The first time I went to the "Frat House," I was chastised for sitting on the wrong color cushion on the sofa. Needless to say, we both resigned and were much happier. During rush week, I saw and heard some things that were shocking. I will not repeat them.

The Mississippi Gulf Coast was only 70 miles from Hattiesburg. We loved to spend time there and would even hitch hike, if necessary. One weekend we decided to go to the coast and talked a friend into taking his car. We assured him it was safe. No sooner had we arrived there, this tall dude from Alabama ask me where I was from. I said Mississippi and he took both hands, shoved them into my chest hard and hit me in the eye.

Not being an experienced fighter, I started wailing away with my head down. It is possible I never hit him. We left that Juke Joint and went to another. Have you ever seen a person who was nice, quiet and polite when sober, but a completely different person when drinking? Amos was like that.

You couldn't ask for a nicer guy, but if he got "tanked up," watch out. We came out of the club and the next thing I knew Amos was walking on the hood of every car there! I just knew they were going to throw us in jail. Thankfully, no one saw him.

After one year at Southern Mississippi, I made the decision to go to Itawamba Junior College (now it's called a community college). Since my major at the time was architecture, one of the required courses was Trigonometry. I hated it (sin, co-sin; tangent co-tangent.) The professor's last name was Mayhall and we called her "Momma." I had a hard time concentrating because she weighed about 300 lbs. When she would write on the chalkboard, the excess fat below who bicep would flop around. I got so tickled it was hard for me not to laugh out loud. She was merciful and gave me a "D."

Itawamba was in Fulton, MS which was about 45 miles away from Aberdeen. It was a free bus ride, so that made it convenient. In order to pass the time we would play Rook. I discovered if I could show my partner my hand by turning my cards face side up, then it was a piece of cake to win. You guessed It. They caught me. It was at Itawamba that I first heard the news that President Kennedy had been shot in Dallas, TX. Like so many people, I will never forget.

After one semester, I decided to take a break from school. I spent 9 months working for my dad. I don't want to mislead you that all I did was work. Aberdeen had a really nice public swimming pool. It had 2 springboards and a tower. The only problem was the deep end of the pool was way too shallow. I saw a guy stand in the deepest place in the pool and hold his arm up. Would you believe you could see his hand.

The tower was 10 feet. One could hit his head on the bottom quite easily. I am genuinely surprised someone didn't get killed. If I wasn't on the golf course, I was at the pool. Did you know that if someone is diving, you can place your hands on the board and right when they spring forward, you can press down really hard on the board and it will shoot them up in the air much higher than normal?

After 9 months of working at the OSS, I was ready to go back to school. Since I liked to draw, I chose Auburn and was majoring in Architecture. Auburn was on the quarter system and when I got there, it was the beginning of the 3rd quarter. The professor kept saying, "As we learned last quarter". The course was Analytic Geometry and Calculus. I was in deep, as I also was taking Greek Mythology. Every class the professor assigned a large reading of "Homer, the Iliad." (I called him "Homer the Idiot." Both courses I hated and went to the finance office and got all but $100.00 back on my tuition. When I showed up at the Rebel Inn, only having been gone about 4 weeks, I was the laughingstock of my friends. Truth of the matter is I didn't know so much math was required for a major in Architecture.

Here we go again back to working for my dad. There were several folks who commuted to Miss. State. As a result, I joined them, and we drove to Starkville daily. Foster Kennedy was a big golfing buddy of mine, but he went to Ole Miss. He came up to me one day and said his mother had read in the newspaper that I had made the Dean's last one semester. She wanted to know if it was a misprint.

Edward Roberts had been in the military and was a fellow commuter. He was 28 years old and was the kind of guy who loved taking a chance. One day it was just Edward and me in his Ford car. He thought he would open her up and see how fast she would go. He got close to 105 miles per hour. I begged him to stop and said that I would walk the rest of the way. He chuckled and said, "Greely, live dangerously, "I LOVE IT." I am sorry to report that Edward only lived to 29. He died in a one car accident. The officers who arrived on the scene said that they couldn't tell who he was nor what kind of car it was.

While at Miss. State, I lived in 2 different dorms. One was named "Hull Hall" and the other was named "Sessums." Man, was Hull Hall loud. There was no carpet and when you closed your door, it sounded like a gun shot. My junior year was spent in Hull with a number of friends.

The school had a beautiful school ring you could purchase for $ 49.50. I had my initials engraved on the inside of it and boy was I glad. I had left it on one of the sinks in the dorm restroom. An honest fellow found it and brought it to me. What a happy camper I was. When the price of gold got to be $17.00 an ounce, I sold it for $300.00. It was locked away in a safe place, besides I couldn't wear it because I was about 50 lbs. heavier than my college days.

Every Sunday night there was a poker game in someone's dorm room. I loved to play poker, but I was really bad at it. My allowance was $ 5.00 per week, since the room and board were already paid. Almost every week I would lose my $ 5.00.

At that time you could buy a vegetable plate for $ .35. I would go to the cafeteria and ask one of my buddies if he would pick up a couple of packages of crackers. (They were free).

When at State, I had a class with a guy named Marcus Roden. He played half back and was superfast. Our fullback was from south Louisiana. To quote John Madden, "He was big and strong and could catch the football, not to mention he could also run over you at 235 lbs." His name was Hoyle Granger. His calves were so large he had to cut his blue jeans before he could get them on. He spoke broken English and struggled with comprehension. Coach called him to his office and wanted to talk about his grades. The first semester he made all "F's" and one "C".

He told the coach, "I must be spending too much time on that one subject". Hoyle was drafted by the Houston Oilers of the AFL and they almost cut him from the roster because he couldn't remember the plays. I'm sure they are glad they didn't because he went on to lead the AFL for several years in a row in rushing.

Fred Barron, our super good middle linebacker, played in the All-Star game in Jackson, MS. We took two car loads to see him play. Someone had brought some alcohol and they were passing the bottle around. The crew made a pit stop and I got out and forearmed a highway sign. My glasses were in the front pocket of my shirt and fell out.

As we made our way to the stadium, I

discovered they had fallen out. I was sick about it and dreaded telling my parents, not to mention I couldn't see the game. On our way back someone said, "Isn't that the sign Greely hit"? We pulled off the road and I walked straight to them. Eureka!! Finding my glasses turned a gloomy day into a sunny day.

MARRIAGE

On February 12, 1967, Shirley and I were joined together in holy matrimony. It was a no-frills wedding with mostly family. Shirley looked beautiful. After the ceremony, we drove to the house, where I had hidden the Chrysler in our basement. I didn't want it to get all painted up with cans tied to the bumper. I was laughing because I thought we had pulled a good switch-a-rue.

It was to our surprise that someone had learned about my deception and had gone to "fix up" the car. There was a "mole" in my company. The car was a mess. They had taken shaving cream and written all over it. We stopped in Montgomery, Al for gas and the service station attendant asked what kind of storm we had been in and we both started giggling.

There was a nice motel close by, so we checked in and prepared for bed. I was so in love! I felt like the luckiest man alive. The room had a vibrating bed for 25 cents. I put a quarter in it and NOTHING. We looked at each other and said, "Oh well, what's a quarter?"

We were awakened about 2 am with the bed vibrating. We both chuckled and went back to sleep. The Florida State fair was in town, so we thought it would be fun. They had one of those "double" Ferris wheels.

I have acrophobia and that wheel stopped us on the highest place possible. Shirley started rocking the seat and I started to turn green. I asked her to please stop, she was scaring me. Later, she told me she was beginning to wonder what kind of a wuss she had married.

Just so you know something of our finances, I borrowed $ 200.00 from dad to be able to go. We were having a wonderful time when our bowels decided not to cooperate. We made a trip to the Rx and purchased every laxative we could find.

MILITARY

In 1967 the Vietnam war was still raging. A friend informed me that my name was high on the draft board. Aberdeen had a National Guard unit and I joined it. I'm so glad I did, even though I did not like military life.

Exactly 2 months had passed since joining and I was off to Ft. Polk, LA. A number of guys went to Leesville, when they got a pass. It also went by the names Fleesville or Diseaseville. When we arrived (went by bus line) at the Reception Station, there was a 3 day wait, before going to our assigned companies.

Some of us were given the job of cleaning the "latrine". I did not even know what it was. The closest thing to showing any interest in army life was I had several small, rubber like green men. It reminds me of the Folgers commercial, "What could be better in the morning than waking up to "soldiers" in your cup," as one little fellow said.

Since I was not "gung-ho" and had not been married but two months, I didn't feel very well. They had a doctor there, and he told me it was my nerves. The food wasn't bad, but I would stand in the line to eat and at the moment I reached the Mess Hall, I would step out line.

Most guys gained weight in Basic Training, but I lost 15 lbs. We were given nice, short haircuts and assigned to company A-3-2. The best thing about the location was it was directly across from the bowling alley, which was air conditioned. Our platoon was under the leadership of a Senior Drill Sargent E-7.

The first week, which did not count toward our training, we took that week to spruce up the place. The first day of official training the DI had the entire company stand in formation. He asked, "How many were college grads." 8 out of 55 stepped forward. Next, he asked how many had taken ROTC? I saw what he was doing, choosing leaders. As a result, I did not raise my hand. He told those who had ROTC to fall back into the formation. Oops, that left only 2 of us. The other man was also given the order to return to the company. Don't ask me why he chose me, but he got about 2 inches from my nose and shouted, "Kirkpatrick, you are the new platoon sergeant. In the morning these floors will be scrubbed, swept, mopped, waxed and buffed by 6AM with no one getting up before 5AM."

I walked out into the open barrack (platoon sergeants) slept in a room of their own) and made my first "talk." I recall someone said, "Hey, Sarg, you have your stripes on upside down."

I told you I was not into being a soldier. The meeting was about getting up at 4 AM and starting to work on the floors. I went to the Supply Clerk to check out how to scrub the floor. He said you couldn't scrum them because they were dyed. Sarg knew it was not possible to do what he was asking. He walked into the barracks and I heard him scream, "Where is that blankety blank Platoon Sargent."

He gave me a real chewing out. After 10 days of listening to guys whine about sore knees, headaches, hang nails and you name it. I went to the DI and he told me he would let me out of the job, if I could find a replacement who wanted it. That was not difficult at all. I knew a guy who would jump on it in an instant. He had a desire to be seen and he readily took over.

I was sent to the 4th squad and was I evermore relived. However, there were several men who were upset with me because they didn't like the new guy. He was somewhat of a jerk, but he made it through the remainder of basic training in the position of platoon sergeant.

There was this one guy who was in the 4th squad. He was so lazy he would wait to the last minute to get out of bed. Since he was in the back of the platoon and it was dark in the early morning, he would turn around and urinate on the ground.

About halfway through basic, we were trained in "puggle stick" fighting. There were several groups, which formed a circle and when you were ready, you would enter the ring and fight. I purposely got in the group with the dude I disliked. When I got close enough to knock his block off, I drew the stick back and he swung an upper cut that caught me square in the chin. Some people call them "fire flies" that dance in your head when you are hit with force.

The blow didn't knock me down, but it definitely dazed me. By the end of basic almost everyone was calling it "Fort Puke, Louseyana". After basic training, those who were going to be Company Clerks went up to Company D-3-4 for training. As far as I was concerned, I never understood hardly any of it. This training was called AIT. Gullible Greely almost fell for the info that said it meant Advanced Infantry Training.

There was a place in Fort Polk called "Tiger Land." It was a simulated village of Vietnam. We used to drive by and see how they lived. It was lunch time and they had on full equipment: steel pot, M16 rifle, backpack, gas mask and rain gear. They stood 6 feet apart at parade rest. We were all thankful that we were not going there.

BECOMING A CHRISTIAN

In April of 1971 I was united with Christ in baptism by faith. It was the result of Jerry Jones and his wife, Wynene, coming to our house for several nights. I had invited my preacher over and he didn't even bring his Bible. Shirley noticed how disappointed I was and said, "Okay, my time." The Joneses came prepared to study.

I could not help but notice Jerry's Bible was well used with markings and writings though out. We all watched a number of "film strips," which started with Genesis and ended with Revelation. It reminds me of the preacher who told the congregation, "Open your Bible and turn to any book, I will be there shortly."

During weeks of study (one night per week) I would ask questions and Jerry would say, "Let's see what the Bible says." I liked that a lot. I don't recall the number of nights, but my heart was touched and I was so happy that God forgave me because I believed (trusted) in Jesus and His work on the cross.

I started reading my Bible and memorizing Scripture. My friends seem to be puzzled by my "strange" behavior. One of my cousins came up to me during a National Guard meeting and said that he had heard I had quit smoking, drinking and cussing. He laughed at me, told me I was going to Hell and walked off. A number of people just couldn't understand why I had changed so much. It gave me an opportunity to try and teach the Gospel (Good news) of God's saving grace because of His great love for us sinners by faith (trust) in the risen Savior.

The death, burial and resurrection of Jesus for our sins is the heart of it all. When a person is united with Christ in the grave of baptism, he/she becomes a new creation (II Cor. 5:17). "Old things have passed away, behold, all things, have become new."

My mom, who I worked with for years, went home at age 99. She wanted to know more about the Bible, so I began to teach her what little I knew. I will never forget the look on her face when she said she was no saint and I said, "I am a saint."

Some people get confused and think a "saint" is someone different from an ordinary Christian. It was almost comical with her knowing some of things I had said and done. After becoming a disciple of Jesus, she was always at the assemblies of the church and studied her Bible every day. She set a wonderful example for my dad.

He spent 4 months in the Tupelo, MS Region Hospital and died with a gaping wound in his chest, but not before his confession and baptism in the hospital. Before his illness, he believed I would take over the business, but I felt I been called into the ministry.

My first cousin, Tommy, worked with me for about 10 years. I so desired he would become a Christian, but he showed no interest. One day I asked him, "How can you come to work every day knowing the Lord could return at any minute?" His answer was typical, "I just don't ever think about it." I am so filled with joy that Tommy became a child of God in 2000. He really has made a great impression on others and he never stops smiling. The Bible says we need to grow up in Christ. This growth will never occur until we become true students of the Word. I like the saying, "We need to get into the Word and let the Word get into us." Praise God for such a savior as Jesus Christ.

In 1976 I uprooted my family, sold our house and moved to Searcy, Arkansas. Shirley and I have often discussed the decision that was made to move. We have always concluded it was the best thing to do.

I received a phone call from Harding CCP

program. I told them I was glad they didn't add another "C" to the name. When I thought about leaving my hometown, I got butterflies in my stomach. Why I didn't even know the books of the Bible. Our oldest son was about 9 when I began to recite the books of the Bible. We did not realize he was listening to my efforts at learning the correct order. One night I said them as fast as I could. He beat me. Would you believe he recited them in 29 seconds and you could understand him!

One beautiful morning we were walking across campus, when we noticed some kids swimming in the pool in front of the Administration building. I said, "Look at that." What kind of parents would allow their children to do such a thing? The closer we got to them, I recognized they were mine! Of course, they had been pushed in by others.

We took the money from the sale of our house in Aberdeen and bought a house in a nice little neighborhood in Searcy. It was approximately 250 miles from Searcy to Aberdeen and every holiday (of any length) we would travel home. The kids liked to play games and sing in the car.

Jerry Jones, who had the same name of the head of the Bible department at Harding, liked for me to preach when we came for a visit, I suppose he enjoyed the short break when I filled in for him. Before leaving for Harding, I preached my first sermon. The Aberdeen church took communion before the sermon. There I was, sitting on the front pew, nervous as a long- tailed cat in a room full of rocking chairs.

My face started to sweat and my mouth got dry. When I reached up to wipe away the sweat, my left temple fell off of my glasses. Oh no! They were still passing the supper, so I asked the young man sitting next to me, if he would get on his hands and knees and look for that tiny screw.

He found it and I began to tighten it with my fingernail. No sooner than I had put it back in the temple, it was time to speak. I told the congregation what had happened and they laughed. It surely was the providence of God. My preparation for the message revealed it was 20 minutes. However, it turned out to be 8 Minutes. This one guy said, "I believe I could have listened 8 more minutes." The church at Aberdeen supported us with $ 600.00 per month. The West Chapel church gave us $50.00 per month for 2 years. We were very grateful for their generosity.

After selling our house in Aberdeen, (actually my mom sold it for us) we packed up and headed for Searcy. It was 250 miles. I rented the largest U-Haul truck they had. About halfway I looked in my rear-view mirror and saw Shirley cross the center line. There was an 18-wheeler headed right at her. Suddenly, Shirley straightened up. When it was convenient to stop, I asked her why she was driving so crazy. She said, "There was a bee in the car!"

We prayed a lot about the transition and was so glad we went. There were some great teachers on the faculty with many years of experience. When people ask me about the school, I often reply, "The worse thing about it is you eventually graduate and have to listen to yourself." Occasionally, I would be speaking and could not remember the word I wanted to use. I tried to laugh about it and that helped.

After the first 8 weeks of school, three of my classmates and I volunteered to go to Iowa for a Campaign for Christ. We would be knocking doors in an effort to set up Bible studies. At least that is what we thought. We came to find out all they wanted us to do was hand out tracts about the church. We were very disappointed and went home 1 day early. We had taken my car, which was a 1972 Chevy. The guys got tickled because it took 12 quarts of oil on a trip of 1200 miles. Someone said, "The next time we stop, tell them to check the gas and fill up the oil."

When the last day came, we were exhausted. Like the fellow who said he had dreamed he was a muffler and woke up "exhausted." One of the men with us didn't know the meaning of quit. He saw a house and begged me to stop. Everyone moaned, but I stopped. He knocked on the door, but no answer. I spotted a huge St. Bernard on the right side of the house. I yelled out to Carl, "I think someone is in the back." Carl had long legs and he locked eyes with the St. Bernard. Carl froze until the dog let out a loud bark and lunged at Carl. I never had seen Carl move that fast, but he was back in the car in what seemed like 3 steps. I know it was wrong of me and I have repented. Carl is such a good guy. He never one time said a word, but just laughed.

There were a few weeks left in school, when the director asked me to preach on a Wednesday night at the College church. My family and I walked to the building. I'm guessing there were 800 in attendance. Shirley and I had visited the congregation a couple of times in the past.

My opening remarks were "If you had told me a few years ago, I would be standing here and preaching, I would have responded with the words of Festus to Paul much learning has made thee mad". (Acts 26:24). I was sure not cross my legs, because we were at church when the speaker, who was sitting on the stage, arose to walk to the pulpit and fell down. It made a huge noise and his face turned red. His leg had fallen asleep and he didn't realize it.

Shirley and I have often talked about what our lives would have been like if we had stayed in Aberdeen. The college there had begun a school of preaching. It was a two-year study of 40 different subjects. One day the family and I were discussing the move to Searcy.

There I was enrolling in a school of preaching school of preaching and didn't even know the books of the Bible. My memory is only average at best. While practicing saying the books out loud, we didn't realize our oldest son (Todd 9) was listening and he asked if he could say them. We were blown away when he said them in 29 seconds, pronouncing them correctly.

The two years at Harding were the best of my life. The college had a media room where we would preach a "mock" sermon and the instructor would video the lesson. Each student was given a critique sheet to give his opinion of how his fellow brother had done.

During one of the men's presentation, I was sitting on the back row, when all of a sudden we heard a loud bang. He had pounded on the pulpit. It was comical to watch every person jump straight up in the air at the same time. The instructor came flying down the stairs, "Don't ever do that unless you let the people know by raising your fist that you are going to hit the pulpit."

I suppose you could cause someone to have a heart attack. It was fun to hear each speaker and try to correct your own mistakes. The incident in the media room reminded me of what happened at Mayflower, AR one Sunday. It was somewhat of an older church and I was preaching along when I came to Ephesians 5:14, "Awake, you who sleep, arise and Christ will give you light." I raised my voice to emphasize the passage, not knowing there was an elderly gentleman who had fallen asleep. He jumped up when I raised my voice and I got so tickled I almost had to stop speaking.

A number of guys preached at relatively small churches every Sunday. For 6 months I co-preached with Robert Cowles at the McIlroy congregation in Arkansas. Bob would speak one Sunday morning and I would speak that night and vice versa. It was about 2 ½ hours from Searcy one way.

Driving home, we always critiqued each other's sermons. Bob was rather long winded to the point that some began to ask which one of us was preaching the morning lesson. They knew if I was preaching, they would be out on time. One Sunday evening, Bob asked me what I thought of his lesson. I told him it was 2 good messages. He laughed. Kudos to Bob for preaching 40 years at the Norwood church in Knoxville TN.

After graduating from Harding School of Biblical Studies we bought a VW bug from a classmate who left the metal emblem on the back, which read, "Christchurch, New Zealand". Also, right in the middle of it was a Kiwi. That emblem generated lots of conversations.

CHURCHES AND PREACHING

The last semester at Harding I accepted a job with the Levy church of Christ in North Little Rock, AK. They were looking for a family to move to south central Mississippi. We would stay and work with the church there and enter the mission field after 1 year. However, it didn't turn out that way. Leon Barnes was the "Pulpit Minister" at Levy and was an outstanding speaker.

He never read from the Bible or from his notes. I think you call it a "photographic" memory. I loved working with him. There were also 2 full time paid elders. Harry McCorkle was one and we made lots of calls together. People would come to the building for food and we would follow up. Someone asked our children what was my job and they answered "substitute preacher."

Before the sermon I was to deliver, one of the Deacons told me to "break a leg." As I made my way to the pulpit, I didn't understand the remark. Later, it was explained to me. It was show business for "do a great job." Levy had just completed building a new auditorium, which would seat about 1,000 people.

The elders asked me to teach the Wednesday night auditorium class. We had been studying, "A Short Life of Christ" in school, so it was easy to put together an 8-week study. The family and I were on our way to the church building when we ran out of gas. I was so embarrassed. My very first class and I'm late. Everyone was looking around wondering where I was. I went to the mic and told the class "That DUMB VW ran out of gas when the gauge said ¼ of a tank." I was never late for another class. I told the class I had a "pass out" for them on the life of Christ. They said, "Don't you mean a "hand out?"

There is a Christian school named Central Arkansas Christian. It was a private school and Leon informed me they needed a teacher for a class of boys in the 7th grade. 20 young men would file into the classroom daily right after PE. I loved those boys, but I had to paddle a couple of them.

They kept pushing the envelope. Finally, I had it with this one fellow, so we made a trip to the next-door classroom. It was the 70's, so you could still spank a kid. I remember lifting him off the floor. He cried until we reached the classroom door and then he put on a big ole smile.

I wanted so much for each young man to make an "A". Therefore, the day before the quiz I would have the test right in front of me. I would read the question and occasionally say, "That would make a great question for tomorrow's test." All of my efforts were in vain, some of the guys still flunked. I felt like a failure.

The book of Acts was our subject and I thoroughly enjoyed teaching. There was this one young man who had a deformity. I don't recall the exact medical name, but he was short and walked with a limp. It was his spine, I think. You know how some people can be abnormal physically, but have a very pleasant disposition? This young fellow was a pleasure to have in class. One morning the phone rang. It was the young man's dad.

His son wanted to be baptized the Bible way. I was excited for him, so I made a mad dash to the hospital, only to learn he was in a body cast up to his neck. Someone came up with a great idea. We could put him in a heavy-duty garbage bag and it would cover his cast completely. You should have seen his smile! The Lord added him to the Book of life, and he will receive a new body, like Christ's body. We sing a lot about heaven in our worship. One hymn is "Won't It Be Wonderful There?" Yes, and I can hardly wait!

After the year at Levy, we were ready for the mission field, or so we thought. Two men I had a great deal of respect for talked with me about becoming the minister for the church in Harrison, AK. Leon had completed preaching in a weeklong meeting there and felt like I would be a good "fit." All through the 2 years at Harding most of the professors warned us about going to a large congregation right after school. The Northside church was about 400 in membership.

I got off on the wrong foot when our daughter (Kelly) went visiting one of our neighbors and told him her brother and dad were in the house drinking beer. Our neighbor believed her and in turn told the waitress, who asked me what I wanted to drink, as I had joined the Kiwanis Club, which met and ate every Monday.

I told her I didn't drink just making a joke. She came back with "That isn't what I heard." It gets worse. My neighbor went to one of my elders and told him what my daughter had said. The elder greatly disappointed me when he came to me and asked if it was true?

Trying to convince Kelly's new friend, she had made it up, I went to his house and spoke with him. It seems that Kelly had been told by her brothers that they were drinking beer. Come to find out, it was ROOT beer. With all seriousness I asked him if he had ever seen the ole TV show "Kids say the darndest things." Also, I asked him if he had seen me on TV, as I was the co-chairman of "Keep Boone County Dry."

After a few weeks, the elder approached me and let me know my neighbor had recanted. What an ordeal, but do you think my neighbor ever apologized to me? There is an old saying I'm reasonably sure you have heard. It goes like this: "Sticks and stones may break my bones, but words will never hurt me."

It was my first and last full-time work. Every day, Monday through Friday we had a 5-minute radio program at 1 PM; a 15-minute radio program every Sunday at 8:30 AM; class on Sunday morning and Sunday evening and a Wednesday evening Bible class at 7:00 PM. Obviously, I was super busy.

Another thing my professors warned us about was having a funeral lesson already prepared. Do you think I did as they suggested? We had been there about 3 months, when one of our deacon's daughter and granddaughter were killed by a drunk driver. The building sat about 600 and there were people standing. I was petrified to say the least. You never know what kind of influence you are having on people. For example, about 25 years had passed and this lady came up to me telling me she had thought about that funeral lesson many times. The truth is, I hardly knew her.

Northside had a group of people who sang at funerals. They were really good, when they were all there. Occasionally, I felt like crawling under the pew the singing was so bad.

After moving to Harrison, I learned the movers had scratched the living room coffee table. I panicked because it was fairly new. Someone suggested I use shoe polish. It was a great suggestion, because we were there for 2 years before the wife found out.

The city of Harrison was about 10 thousand located in northwest Arkansas. It is a beautiful place with a "Town Square" right in the middle. After about 10 years, I felt it would be refreshing to move. I received a phone call from the University church in Conway, Arkansas. One Sunday morning they sent 2 men to hear a sermon. They didn't tell me they were coming and I liked that. It is my opinion that if you don't let the preacher know you are coming, you will hear him on a "normal" Sunday. I believe it was Thomas Cromwell who said to his portrait painter, "Paint me warts and all."

Have you ever heard a preacher who had a different voice when he entered the pulpit? I went to school with a fellow who had only one style of preaching. He elevated his voice to a rather high level and stayed there the entire sermon. Most of my classmates told him to pause at times and come down to give the church a break. His answer was, "I can't preach any other way."

While at Harding, there was a course named "Sermon Preparation". It was followed by another course named "Sermon Delivery." The school had a great media room where they taped speeches. You talk about being nervous and anxious. The professor would write down what you said or did and share it with you and your classmates.

One of my friends scratched his face about 20 times and didn't even remember it. I used words like, "winder, dea'th (2 syllables), manner, and idear. Also, we "carry" things in Mississippi. We carry our child to the Doctor. We carry our car to the shop. We carry the bus to a meeting. One time I announced we were "carrying" the bus to this town about 30 miles away and after the assembly, one of the deacons said, "I hope there is a good turnout." I agreed. He continued, "It's gonna take a heap of us to carry the bus that far!" I got my revenge when I read the Israelites were "carried" away into Babylonian captivity.

While living in Harrison, AK, our children enjoyed playing sports. One year all three Todd, Heath and Kelly had a ball game on the same day and same time. Todd enjoyed playing American Legion baseball. He got to where he was a pretty good pitcher. Heath decided he would end his career at Pony league baseball. Kelly loved softball, but her face would get so red it concerned me. Todd owns his own business: A-1 Home Inspection in Springfield, MO. Heath is a preacher at Woodland Heights in Harrison, AK. He has grown the congregation from 40 to about 600. He is without a doubt the best speaker I have ever heard.

Kelly owned her own hair salon for several years, but burned out and chose to move to the Azores Islands. The cities are old and beautiful, belonging to Portugal. Shirley and I had the pleasure of visiting her a couple of years ago. We had a great time. The scenery and the food were incredible.

When Heath was growing up, he was a huge Minnesota Vikings fan, while Todd loved the Dallas Cowboys. Harding invited Fran Tarkington to speak one night, so Heath and I went to hear him. We hung around and shook his hand. I was surprised that he and I were the exact same size. Fran played pro football at QB for 17 years and still holds a number of records. Heath tried his hand at football, but broke his arm in the 6th grade.

I mentioned my sister and her husband earlier, Bill and Brenda Harrington. Brenda taught school until she retired. We were not that close during our younger years, but as we grew older, we got closer. Brenda graduated from MSCW in Columbus, MS in elementary education. She probably laughs as much as anyone I know.

Bill was a big guy standing 6’6” and 250. He was a nice-looking man with a head full of salt and pepper hair and it stayed thick until his death. He had bone cancer and lived beyond the expected date. He and I were great friends and because of our love for golf, we went to the Masters practice rounds in Augusta, GA three times.

It was Wednesday, when they had the Par 3 tournament at 1 PM. I was tired from walking the course that morning. There was a natural slope that was perfect for lying down and taking a power nap. I had barely fallen asleep, when I felt someone slightly shaking me. I heard this voice saying, “Sir, there is no lying down at the

Masters." Bill said he saw the official approaching me and laughed when I finally figured out what had happened. He told me he had told that story numerous times.

One of the highlights one year was when V.J. Sing made a hole in one by skipping his ball across the water on hole 16. The funniest thing was Darren Clark (smoking a cigar and wearing gold pants) hit 3 balls from the regular tee and walked to the edge of the water with the crowd yelling, "Skip, Skip, Skip." He wanted to accommodate the patrons, so he dropped a ball and flew the water. I heard a loud voice say, "Hey Darren, you are supposed to hit the water."

Darrin looked all around and found the fellow. He then motioned for him to come to him. The guy was hesitant at first, but finally mustered up the courage to go. Darrin handed him his club, dropped a ball and said fire away. The poor man just about killed someone behind the green. He didn't get close to the water. When we returned home, I got on our computer and someone had taken a camera, filmed the incident and posted it on U Tube. As I was panning the scene, I spotted us sitting in the stadium seats. If you like golf, you would love the practice rounds. There is a lottery where you sign up (Masters.com) every year and they randomly select who goes. TV does not do the Masters course justice.

After spending almost 12 years at Northside, I resigned. It was sad, but I was "burned out" as some say. We said our "goodbyes" and headed north for Springfield, MO. Our oldest son had married and had a son of his own. We thought we could offer our help. I have never seen a child who looked exactly like his dad.

When each was 2 years old, we found some pictures of Kevin and Todd and you could not tell them apart. Our efforts to help, unfortunately, were in vain, but everyone who knew us, knew we had tried our best. The church in Harrison had given us a check for severance pay thanks to Flavil Yeakly, Jr. who drove up from Searcy and served as an arbitrator. We were pleasantly surprised to receive a check.

We arrived in Springfield Dec. 30th 1990. When we left Harrison, I was wearing a tee shirt. The next morning the ground was covered with snow and ice. All of our appliances froze overnight. I walked out the front door with Kevin in my arms and that is the first time I've seen my feet over my head, as I slipped the ice while going out the front door. It stayed on the ground for a couple of weeks and the back roads for weeks.

WORK

I was used to getting up and going to work. The Lord knew this and I found a selling job. I had some experience in outside sales, when I worked for my dad. I was elated to be hired by Springfield Paper Company. One thing I really liked was there were about 5 thousand items in our catalog with toilet paper being the best seller.

I was fortunate to have taken over an already established route. I loved my GM, Paul Todd. He had a great personality, but was a better salesman than a GM. He had some customers he had called on for years. I remember this one lady who owned "Aunt Martha's Pancake House." I called on her every week.

One week I stopped by, as usual. The cook was new and told me the napkin supply was fine. It wasn't and she ran out. The boss called me into his office, told me to sit down and proceeded to tell me he had received a call from Aunt Martha. One reason I loved him was he told me not to worry about it because he would handle it. Later, I learned she had asked Paul to fire me!

Randy Staples was my truck driver and in 25 years we never one time had a cross word with each other. Randy was the hardest working man I have ever known. Always jovial, smiling and laughing. He also rarely made a mistake. One thing he did make was money for me. He would deliver to the back door, while I called on the customer at the front door. Randy convinced me to keep going to Branson one day a week. It was a great suggestion! We took both backseats out of my van and just about filled it every Thursday. The company truck would follow me on Monday. A huge plus for working the city of Branson was the number of complimentary tickets you got.

There is a true story I tell where the Dragon Inn Chinese Restaurant ordered some rice cups and lids. One day at lunch the phone rang for me. It was the owner and he sounded upset. He said, "Mr. Reely, you send me wrong lice cup. It is right size, but it says, "Fish Bait" on it with a picture of worms. The number he ordered was 8SJ20. I had not worked there but a few months and mistakenly sent him a 8SJ20B. I had no clue what the "B" stood for, but I found out when he said, "You bring me right cup, right now!"

While working full time at the paper company,

I also preached and we lived in Sparta, MO. It was a church of about 130 people. It wasn't easy working a secular job, preaching twice on Sunday and teaching the auditorium class, along with teaching a teen class on Wednesday night. It was my "Sweetheart" church for 9 years.

Those folks were the salt of the earth. Once again I was getting very tired and thought a Sabbatical was needed. I don't recall how long I went without preaching, but the church at Fordland was looking for a "part-time" man to fill the pulpit. We had moved to Nixa, MO, so it was not a lengthy distance, only about thirty miles one way.

Shirley and I enjoyed meeting new friends and you could not ask to be treated any better. I have often said that when you move, you don't lose your old friends, you just add your new friends to your old ones. It's amazing how many Christian friends you can love. Sometimes I tell folks, "Listen, I have been on both sides of the fence, and I can tell you without any hesitation, the Christian side is far, far, far better". Neal Pyror (Bible) professor at Harding, (gone to his reward) used to say, "All this, meaning this earth and heaven too!"

Randy Staples convinced me to keep going to Branson one day a week after my retirement at age 65. What a great suggestion. We took both back seats out of my van and just about every week we would fill it up. The company truck would follow me on Monday, after I had gone down to Branson on Thursday. A huge plus for working the city of Branson was the number of complimentary tickets you got.

AUTHOR'S NOTE:

I hope you enjoyed these stories. I'm sure I forgot some things, but hopefully there are not too many errors in the stories. I had no idea how difficult it would be to write a book and have it published.

Made in the USA
Middletown, DE
11 November 2022